1000 basic spellings

Text: Alan Dury

Design: Andrew Maddock

Published in Great Britain by World International Publishing Limited,
an Egmont Company, Egmont House,
PO Box III, Great Ducie Street,
Manchester M60 3BL.

Printed in Finland.
ISBN 0 7498 1501 9

A catalogue record for this book is available from the British Library.

To the student

English has become the most widely spoken language in the world, but that doesn't make it an easy one to write. Saying words and understanding what they mean is much easier than spelling them.

One problem is that there are few spelling rules, and often, the same sound can be spelt in several ways.

To improve our spelling we need to find out all we can about the 26 letters of the alphabet and the sounds they make.

the vowels: a, e, i, o, u

These five letters are called vowels. Vowels form the main sound of all words and all words contain at least one vowel. Sometimes the letter 'y' acts as a vowel too.

the consonants

There are 21 consonants in the English alphabet. Some make only one sound. Others, such as 'c', 'g' and 's' can make a variety of sounds.

Sometimes two consonants or two vowels stand together and combine to make a single sound such as the 'sh' in 'shop' or the 'ea' in 'tea'.

When letters are doubled as in 'apple' and 'foot', these double letters do not always form the same sound. The words 'foot', 'food' and 'flood' for example, are all spelt with 'oo' yet they each sound very different.

There are some words where a letter is 'silent'. This makes spelling especially difficult. The 'b' in 'dumb' and 'w' in 'wring', are two examples.

We will also learn about the magic 'e' which makes a short vowel sound such as the 'i' in 'fin' into a long vowel sound as in 'fine'.

There are also some words that sound the same but are not spelt the same way and their meanings are very different, too. For example, the hair on your head is not the same as the small furry animal called a hare. A cupboard could be described as being bare but this is not the same as a bear who lives in the wild.

This book starts by looking at the vowel sounds — that is the main sound of a word. It then goes on to the sounds consonants make, both alone and in combination with each other. You can use this book as a reference by finding the particular spelling problem you have with a word and checking it under its sound. Or you can work through it from beginning to end.

Another way of learning how to spell new words is to use the Spelling Code. There are four steps to this:

1. LOOK
2. COVER
3. WRITE
4. CHECK

1. LOOK at the word carefully and try to remember it.
2. COVER up the word.
3. WRITE the word without copying it.
4. CHECK the word to see if you are right.

If you get the spelling right, move on to the next word. If you get it wrong, try that word again using the four simple stages as before.

Remember, learning anything takes time. The rules in this book will help you understand letter groups and their sounds. As your spelling improves you will be able to use these rules when you learn new words.

The Vowel Sounds

These sounds are made from the letters A, E, I, O and U.
The letter Y can sometimes be a vowel, too.

Vowel sounds can be short or long.

bat (short 'a')
bate (long 'a')

These words have the 'ai' sound as in 'hair'.

air
bear
fare
their
there

They all have the same sound but are spelt differently.

These words have the 'ai' spelling as in 'air'.

chair
fair
flair
hair
lair
pair
stair

4

These have the 'ea' spelling.

pear
tear
wear

These have the 'are' spelling.

care
dare
fare
mare
rare

The 'eir' and 'ere' spelling when it sounds like 'air' is not very common.

heir
where

Write more 'ai' sounds here.

The short 'a' sound

Here are some words which sound like 'man' with a short vowel.

ban

can

fan

pan

ran

tan

van

But 'wander' sounds more like 'on' in 'pond'.

The long 'a' sound

The 'a' sound as in 'car' or 'tomato' can be spelt in different ways.

Here the words are spelt with 'as'.

class

fast

last

mast

past

task

They can also have 'al' in them.

calf

half

The 'ar' spelling is more common.

bar
card
far
hard
jar
larder
park
star

Some words are spelt with 'ath'.

father
lather
rather

The 'au' spelling appears in:

laugh
laughter

Write more long 'a' sounds here,
for example:

daft

The 'aw' sound

Here are some words with the 'aw' sound as in 'morning'.

bought
chalk
daughter
hall
law
oar
order
war

That's eight different spellings for the same sound.

Here are some with 'ough'.

fought
nought
ought
sought
wrought

The 'al' spelling is easier.

balk
talk
walk

Here are some with 'augh'.

caught
taught

But 'all' is more common:

ball
call
fall
stall
wall

All these words have the 'aw' spelling for the sound.

dawn
gnaw
jaw
paw
raw
saw
spawn
yawn

The letters 'oar' appear in these.

boar
roar
soar
uproar

These words are spelt with 'or'.

border
chord
cord
fork
lord
sword

The 'ar' spelling as in 'war' is an exception.

Write more 'aw' sounds here.

The 'ay' sound

Here are some words with the 'ay' sound as in 'day'.

clay
date
drain
eight
steak
whey

That's six different ways of spelling the same sound.

Here are some words with 'ay'.

day
fray
may
pay
say

The 'ay' sound as in 'date' can be followed by different consonants.

ape
cage
fake
gale
late
pane
rave
safe

These words have 'ai' in them as in 'drain'.

again
brain
chain
fail
jail
main
plain
rain
train

The 'ei' and 'ea' spellings to make this sound are not common.

neighbour
weigh

break
great

'ey' is in these words:

grey
prey

The short 'e' sound

The 'e' sound as in 'bell' can be spelt 'ea' and 'ay' as well.

Here the 'e' can be followed by different consonants.

bed
dent
fell
hedge
lemon
present
wet
zebra

The same sound is spelt 'ea' in these words.

bread
dread
head
heavy
lead (a metal)
pleasant
zealot

Don't forget that the 'ay' in 'says' has the same sound.

The 'ear' sound

All these words have an 'ear' sound as in 'dear'.

> **appear**
> **career**
> **here**
> **pier**
> **weird**

That's five different ways of spelling the same sound, though the last two are not very common.

Here are some words spelt 'ear'.

> **clear**
> **ear**
> **fear**
> **gear**
> **hear**
> **near**
> **rear**
> **spear**
> **weary**

These are spelt with 'eer'.

beer
deer
leer
queer
steer
veer

These words are spelt with 'er'.

mere
query

The 'ier' spelling is most often found in comparative adjectives.

cosy	cosier
misty	mistier
pretty	prettier
silly	sillier
wary	warier

Write more 'ier' spellings here.

The long 'ee' sound

The 'ee' sound as in 'feet' can have several spellings.

ceiling
chief
female
key
magazine
neat
people (You'll have to learn this exception.)
queen
scene

Write more long 'ee' sounds here, for example:

mean
street

The 'i' before 'e' rule

That's nine different ways of spelling the 'ee' sound.

There's a rule for the first one – the 'i' before 'e' rule, except after 'c'.

These words follow that rule and have the 'ee' sound.

conceive

deceive

perceive

receive

These are all 'i' before 'e' words. Remember the word must have the 'ee' sound.

believe

brief

field

relieve

shield

thief

One common exception is: seize. These words have their 'ee' sound spelt with a single 'e'.

demon

immediate

medium

obedient

previous

senior

tedium

The 'ey' or 'y' spelling of the 'ee'
sound is more common at the end of a
word.

duty
funny
happy
monkey
smithy
trusty
zippy

In these words, the 'ee' sound is spelt
'ine'.

machine
morphine
sardine
sleepiness
weariness

Write more 'ine' spellings here.

Here, the same sound is spelt 'ea'.

beat
eat
heat
meat
pleat
treat
wheat
zeal

In these words, the spelling is the same as the sound.

bee
bleed
creep
feet
free
green
keen
meet
sleep
three

These words have the 'ee' sound spelt 'ene'.

gene
obscene
scenery

These words have an 'er' sound, as in 'alert'.

bird
earn
journey
mercy
purse
worse

Six ways of spelling the 'er' sound.

These words spell it as in 'bird'.

birth
dirt
first
girl
girth
twirl

Here, the 'er' sound is spelt 'ea' as in 'earn'.

hearse
learn
pearl
yearn

Here, the 'er' sound is spelt 'our'.

courageous
courtesy
journal

It can also be spelt 'er'.

bigger
copper
dinner
ever
finer
her
infernal
kernel
ladder
modern
never
November
pepper
robber
shelter

Write more 'er' spellings here.

In these words, the 'er' sound is spelt 'ur'.

burn
burst
curve
departure
failure
furniture
future
nurse
return

Here, the 'er' sound is spelt 'or'.

exterior
horror
interior
mayor
radiator
stubborn
word

The short 'i' sound

These words have the sound 'i' as in 'bit'.

build
hymn
pig

Can you find any more words which use the 'ui' spelling?
Here's one:

guinea

The 'y' spelling for this sound is not common, either.

pyramid
bicycle
Egypt

All these words use the 'i' spelling.

bid
did
fib
hid
ill
kill
king
mill
pin
six
thing
wing

The long 'i' sound

These words have the 'i' sound as in 'five'.

> **alive**
> **die**
> **eye**
> **fight**
> **style**

That's five different spellings for the same sound.

These words all use the 'i' spelling as in 'alive'.

> **blind**
> **dime**
> **diver**
> **idle**
> **kite**
> **knife**
> **sign**
> **wine**

These words use the 'ie' spelling as in 'die'.

> **cries**
> **flies**
> **pie**
> **tries**

These words use the 'ye' spelling as in 'eye'.

dye
goodbye
stye

And these have 'igh' as in 'sigh'.

alight
high
light
might
night
right
sight

These words have the 'y' spelling and the 'y' is the vowel in each case as in 'style'.

cry
dry
fly
my
spy
why

The short 'o' sound

The 'o' sound you hear in 'frog' is usually spelt with an 'o', but there are some exceptions.

cough
knowledge
sausage
wasp
what

The following words follow the rule.

bottom
cross
hot
long
not
pot
rot
shop
stop
top

But don't forget 'what' and 'yacht' which are like 'wasp' above.

And 'because' is spelt like 'sausage'.

The long 'o' sound

The 'o' sound you hear in 'hold' can be spelt in five ways.

blow
cone
float
sew
toe

These words use the 'ow' spelling as in 'blow'.

arrow
below
borrow
follow
mallow
shallow
sparrow
tomorrow
yellow

Write more 'ow' spellings here.

These words use the 'o' spelling as in 'cone'.

bone
home
joke
lone
phone
rope
stone
yoyo
zone

These words use the 'oa' spelling as in 'float'.

boat
goal
loan
moan
moat
soap

The 'ew' spelling for this sound is exceptional. Can you find any more like 'sew'?

Here the sound is spelt 'oe' as in 'toe'. These words are usually the plurals of words ending in 'o'.

cargoes
doe
echoes
floe
heroes
mosquitoes
oboe
potatoes
tomatoes
volcanoes

Write more 'oe' spellings here.

The 'ore' sound

The 'ore' sound you hear in 'door' can be spelt in three ways.

poor
sure
tour

These words have the 'oo' spelling as in 'poor'.

floor
moor

These words have the 'ur' spelling as in 'sure'.

cure
demure
lure
mature
pure

These words have the 'ou' spelling as in 'tour'.

tourism
tournament

The 'ow' sound

The 'ow' sound you hear in 'crown' can either be spelt 'ow', or 'ou' as in 'foul'.

These words use the 'ow' spelling as in 'crown'.

allow
brown
clown
down
frown
power
tower
town

These words use the 'ou' spelling as in 'foul'.

aloud
around
cloud
found
loud
pound
round
scout
sound
thousand

The 'oi' sound

The 'oy' sound you hear in 'joy' can also be spelt 'oi' as in 'spoil'.

These words use the 'oy' spelling as in 'joy'.

boy
coy
loyal
toy

Can you find any more?
These words use the 'oi' spelling as in 'spoil'.

boil
coil
coin
foil
moist
noise
oil
soil
toil

The short 'u' sound

The 'u' sound you hear in 'luck' is spelt most often in three ways.

> **bun**
> **honey**
> **nation**

And sometimes as in 'flood', 'does' or 'young'.

These words all have the 'u' spelling as in 'bun'.

> **buck**
> **cut**
> **duck**
> **dumb**
> **fun**
> **lung**
> **muck**
> **rung**
> **sung**
> **truck**

Write more 'u' spellings here.

These words all have the 'o' spelling as in 'honey'.

come
kingdom
money
seldom
some

'ion' at the end of a word has the same sound as in 'nation':

lotion
potion
ration
satisfaction

This word has the 'oo' spelling:

blood

Can you find any more?

The 'u' sound you hear in 'put' has three main spellings.

could
full
wood

It can sometimes be spelt with 'o' as in 'wolf'.

These words both have the 'ou'
spelling as in 'could'.

should
would

These words have the 'u' spelling as
in 'full'.

bush
cushion
push

These words have the 'oo' spelling as
in 'wood'.

book
cook
crook
foot
good
hook
look
rook
soot
took

'

The long 'u' sound

The long 'u' sound you hear in 'rude' has seven spellings.

blue
boot
flew (This is different from 'y + ew' in 'new'.)
fruit
group
move
rule

These words use the 'oo' spelling as in 'boot'.

hoot
root
school
shoot
too
tool
zoo

These words use the 'ue' spelling as in 'blue'.

clue
cue
flue
glue
queue
rue

The 'ew' sound

This word has the 'ew' spelling as in 'flew'.

jewel

These words have the 'ui' spelling as in 'fruit'.

juice
recruit

These words have the 'ou' spelling as in 'group'.

coup
croup
crouton
soup

These words have the 'o' spelling as in 'move'.

do
to
who

These words have the 'u' spelling as in 'rule'.

flute
juke-box

The 'you' sound

The 'y + ew' ('you') sound in 'new' has four main spellings.

dew
onion
use
yet

These words are all spelt with 'ew' as in 'dew'.

few
hew
mew
pew
stew

The 'io' spelling as in 'onion' is usually at the end of a word. Sometimes it can be spelt 'ia' or 'iu'.

billion
hessian
million
opium
simian
trillion

These words all have the 'u' spelling
as in 'use'.

curious
duty
fury
lurid
putrid
spurious
stupid

All words beginning with 'y' as well,
such as 'yet', have the same sound.

yacht
yam
yard
yellow
yes
yeti

Don't forget 'Europe' which has the
same 'y + ew' sound but is spelt
differently. 'Eureka!' is another one.

The Magic 'e'

Adding the letter 'e' to the end of a word can change the sound of the vowel in front, even though the final 'e' is not pronounced.

This is called the magic 'e'.

Short 'a' sound becomes long 'a' sound.

cap + e = cape
fat + e = fate
gap + e = gape
hat + e = hate
man + e = mane
pan + e = pane
rat + e = rate
tap + e = tape

Short 'i' sound becomes long 'i' sound.

dim + e = dime
din + e = dine
fin + e = fine
pin + e = pine
quit + e = quite
rip + e = ripe
strip + e = stripe
writ + e = write

Short 'o' sound becomes long 'o' sound.

cod + e = **code**
dot + e = **dote**
hop + e = **hope**
lob + e = **lobe**
not + e = **note**
rob + e = **robe**

Short 'u' sound becomes long 'u' sound.

cut + e = **cute**
tub + e = **tube**

Write more magic 'e' spellings here.

The Consonant Sounds

The letter 'b' at the end of a word is silent when there is an 'm' in front of it, so don't forget to include it in these words.

bomb
comb
thumb
tomb
womb

Double 'b' in the middle of a word can change the length of the vowel in front.

robber
robot (long 'o' sound and short 'o' sound in the same word)

The double consonant usually has a short vowel in front of it.

short	long
daddy	lady
flipper	pipe
hammer	tame
happy	cape
poppy	pope
rubber	ruby

The letter 'b'

The letter 'b' can join other consonants in these combinations at the beginning of a word.

bl	br
black	brave
bleat	break
bliss	bright
bloom	brother
blunt	brush

'b' can also combine with any vowel at the beginning of a word.

bad
bed
bit
bow
bus
byte

The letter 'c'

The letter 'c' can be soft as in 'city' or hard as in 'camera'.

The soft letter 'c' sounds like an 's' and must have 'e', 'i' or 'y' after it.

> **cell**
> **centre**
> **cinema**
> **citrus**
> **cycle**
> **Cyprus**

The hard letter 'c' sounds more like a 'k'.

> **café**
> **cart**
> **conifer**
> **conker**
> **cuckoo**
> **curtain**

These words have the same hard sound but are spelt with a 'k'.

> **kangaroo**
> **kennel**
> **kipper**
> **koala**
> **kung fu**

The letter 'c' can join other consonants at the beginning of a word in these combinations.

ch	chr
champion	**Christmas**
check	**chrome**
chimney	**chrysalis**
chocolate	
church	

cl	cr
clam	**crab**
clever	**cream**
climb	**crisp**
clot	**cross**
club	**crust**

This same sound can have different spellings in the middle of a word.

account
echo
luck
cheque

These words have a double 'c' as in 'account'.

accordion
raccoon
succour

This word has 'ch' as in 'echo'. Can you find any more?

school

These words have 'ck' as in 'luck'.

bucket
docker
duck
lock
racket
suck
tacky

These words have 'qu' as in 'cheque'.

bouquet
croquet
opaque

The letter 'd'

The letter 'd' is doubled in these words.

bid	bidder
bud	budding
hid	hidden
mad	madder
sad	sadder

'd' can join 'r' at the beginning of a word:

dragon
dress
drip
drop
drum
dry

The combination 'dge' is in the middle of a word. This sounds the same as a soft 'g' at the beginning of words such as 'giant' and 'ginger'. It also has the same sound as a 'j'.

dodge	jam
fudge	jelly
judge	jig
nudge	jolly

The letter 'f'

The sound 'f' makes in 'fat' has these spellings.

cough
fish
giraffe
half
photo

These words have the 'gh' spelling as in 'cough'.

enough
laugh

These words have the 'f' spelling as in 'fish'.

face
faint
feed
fell
field
finish
flat
fog
frog
funny
fuzzy

These words have a double 'f' as in 'giraffe'.

afford
coffee
jiffy
staff
toffee
waffle

The silent 'l' before the 'f' as in 'half' is also in:

calf

These words have the 'ph' spelling of the 'f' sound as in 'photo'.

cipher
pheasant
physics
telephone

Write more 'ph' spellings here.

The letter 'g'

The sound 'g' makes in 'get' has three spellings.

> go
> ghost
> foggy

The double 'g' as in 'foggy' is usually in the middle of a word. Except for: 'egg'.

These words have the 'g' spelling as in 'go'.

> gap
> gear
> girl
> goal
> grasp
> gun

These words have the 'gh' spelling as in 'ghost'.

> Ghana
> gherkin
> ghoul

These words have a double 'g' as in 'foggy'.

> bigger
> muggy
> soggy

50

Words can also be spelt with a single 'g' in the middle or at the end.

bug
igloo
wigwam
zigzag

The letter 'g' can be hard or soft like the letter 'c'.

'g' has a soft sound when 'e', 'i' or 'y' comes after it:

engine
gem
gentle
giant
gypsy
gyroscope

'g' has a hard sound in these words:

gasp
gone
gull

'g' can join the consonants 'l', 'n' and 'r':

glove
gnat
grit

The 'gn' here is pronounced 'n':

gnome
gnu

The letter 'h'

The letter 'h' is often silent.

heir
honest
honour
hour

It can combine with 'r' in these words, but you don't hear it.

rhino
rhyme
rhythm

In these words, it combines with 'w' and is still silent.

whack
what
wheel
where
whip
whisky
why

Write more 'wh' spellings here.

Be careful with the letter 'l'. These words end in a single 'l'

beautiful
careful
hopeful
tearful
wistful

because they're all adjectives. When they become adverbs, double the 'l'.

beautifully
carefully
hopefully
tearfully
wistfully

Sometimes the 'l' is difficult to hear, but it's still there.

balm
calm
chalk
palm
talk
walk

The letters 'm' and 'n'

Doubling the letters 'm' and 'n' often shortens the vowel in front as we have seen.

dime	dimmer
lame	stammer
same	hammer
sane	spanner

The letter 'n' can be silent when it follows an 'm', as can the letter 'b' in 'lamb'.
Can you hear the 'n' in these words?

autumn

condemn

solemn

Here the letter doubles without changing the sound of the vowel.

pen	pennant
gun	gunner
run	runner
sin	sinner
sum	summer
win	winner

In words such as these, where the letter 'k' is in front of 'n', the 'k' is always silent.

knack

knee

knife

knock

knuckle

Don't forget to write it!

The letter 'p'

The letter 'p' is silent when it's in front of 'n', 's' or 't'.

pneumonia

psychology

pterodactyl

The letter 'q'

The letter 'q' is always linked to a 'u', whether it's at the beginning, in the middle or at the end of a word.

quack

question

quiet

quote

delinquent

inquiry

sequence

appliqué

pique

The letter 's'

The letter 's' is sometimes silent.

aisle
island
isle

The 's' sound you hear in 'September' can have four spellings.

ice
kiss
science
sister

These words have the 'ce' spelling as in 'ice'.

dice
mice
rice
thrice
vice

These words have the double 's' spelling as in 'kiss'.

governess
hiss
miss
mistress
posse
possess

56

These words have the 'sc' spelling as in 'science'.

> **scenario**
> **scene**
> **scenery**
> **scent**

These words have the 's' spelling as in 'sister'.

> **base**
> **basin**
> **case**
> **disease**
> **fist**
> **mister**

'se' or 'ce'

Sometimes you can hear the difference.

> **advice**   **advise**

The rule is that the noun is spelt 'ce' and the verb 'se'.

> **licence**   **license**
> **practice**   **practise**

My advice is don't forget to practise your spelling!

The 'sh' sound

The 'sh' sound you hear in 'shoe' can have several spellings.

> **chic**
> **mention**
> **precious**
> **shut**
> **sure**
> **tension**

The 'ch' spelling is in words such as:

> **cache**
> **chicane**
> **machine**

Be careful with 'sion' and 'tion' as they both sound the same.

> **confusion** **caution**
> **invasion** **fraction**
> **mission** **nation**
> **pension** **ration**

These words have the 'ci' spelling..

> **spacious**
> **vicious**

These words have the 'sh' spelling.

> **dish**
> **fashion**
> **fish**
> **push**
> **sash**
> **shame**
> **show**

The letter 't'

Sometimes the letter 't' is silent when it comes after 's' in the middle of a word.

> **fasten**
> **listen**
> **mistletoe**
> **trestle**
> **whistle**

The letter 'w' is also silent when it comes before 'r' and sometimes when it's before 'h'.

> **wrap**
> **wrestle**
> **wriggle**
> **write**
> **wrong**
> **who**
> **whole**

The Apostrophe

The apostrophe can be used for two purposes.

I. To show 'belonging'.

This is John's book.

The apostrophe tells you that the book belongs to John.

If the name already ends in an 's', the apostrophe still goes in the same place.

Can I borrow Chris's bike?

2. To show where there are one or more letters missing when two words have been made into one.

I'm	=	I am
you're	=	you are
he's	=	he is
we're	=	we are
they're	=	they are
I've	=	I have
who've	=	who have

Remember: 'it's' can either mean
'it is' or 'it has'.
You should be able to tell
from the other words.

It's raining. = It is raining.
It's rained. = It has rained.

This happens with 'he's', 'she's',
'who's', etc.

Note: the word 'its' has no apostrophe
when the 'belonging' sense is used.

That's a nice dog.
What is its name?

You will have to be careful with these
words which sound the same.

they're and **their** and **there**

you're and **your**

it's and **its**

who's and **whose**

Plurals

To make most words plural, you add an 's'.

cat   cats

If the word already ends in 's', you add 'es'.

gas   gases
loss   losses

Other words that add 'es' in the plural are: words ending in 'o'

domino   dominoes
echo   echoes
potato   potatoes
tomato   tomatoes

words ending in 'ch'

latch   latches
stitch   stitches

words ending in 'sh'

fish   fishes
wish   wishes

words ending in 'x'

tax   taxes

words ending in 'z'

buzz   buzzes
fizz   fizzes

Some words ending in 'f' or 'fe'
change the 'f' to 'v' before adding 'es'.

calf	calves
half	halves
knife	knives
leaf	leaves
life	lives
loaf	loaves
thief	thieves
wife	wives

Words ending in 'y' drop the 'y' and
add 'ies' when the letter before the 'y'
is a consonant.

city	cities
duty	duties
fly	flies

But...

boy	boys
joy	joys
toy	toys

And of course, some words change
completely.

child	children
foot	feet
man	men
mouse	mice
tooth	teeth
woman	women

Some don't change at all, as with 'sheep'.

Months of the Year

January
February
March
April
May
June
July
August
September
October
November
December

Days of the Week

Monday
Tuesday
Wednesday
Thursday
Friday
Saturday
Sunday